Never Ask A Man
the
Size of His Spread

Never Ask A Man *t h e* Size of His Spread

A Cowgirl's Guide To Life

Gladiola Montana

GIBBS·SMITH
→P
PUBLISHER

SALT LAKE CITY

First edition
96 95 94 93   10 9 8 7 6 5 4

The quotations in this book come from a mixture of lore and experience.

This is a Peregrine Smith Book, published by
Gibbs Smith, Publisher
P.O. Box 667
Layton, UT 84041

Design by Mary Ellen Thompson, TTA Design
Illustrations by Bonnie Cazier, © 1993 by Gibbs Smith, Publisher:
cover, pp. 2, 4, 6, 8, 10, 12, 14, 18, 20, 22, 24, 30, 32, 40, 42, 46,
48, 52, 54, 56, 66, 72, 76, 80, 86, 94, 96, 104, 108, 114, 116, 118,
122, 124, 126, 130, 132, 134, 136, 138
Illustrations by Thomas J. Sanker, © 1993 by Gibbs Smith, Publisher:
pp. 1, 16, 28, 36, 38, 44, 50, 58, 60, 62, 64, 68, 100, 102, 106, 128
Illustrations by Will James (from *Cowboys North and South*, Charles
Scribner's Sons, © 1924), pp. 70, 78, 84, 88, 112
Animation by Richard Haight, © 1993 by Gibbs Smith, Publisher
Cover photograph by Robert Casey, © 1993 by Gibbs Smith, Publisher

Manufactured in the U. S. A.

Library of Congress Cataloging-in-Publication Data
Montana, Gladiola.
Never ask a man the size of his spread : a cowgirl's guide to life / Gladiola
Montana.
p. cm.
ISBN 0-87905-554-5 (pbk.)
1. Cowgirls—West (U.S.)—Humor. I. Title.
F596.M655 1993
978-dc20   92-43920
                                      CIP

THE CODE OF HER WEST

Use a short rope,
a sweet smile,
and a hot brand.

Callin' women the
weaker sex makes
about as much sense
as callin' men the
stronger one.

1

Whether a horse turns out to be a good cow horse or a poor one pretty much depends on the intelligence of the handler.

When a cowboy gives
you a key to his truck,
you know you're
close to winning the
key to his heart.

A woman who intends
to lean on her husband
for support
better be sure
he stands on solid
ground.

Anybody who thinks
they know everything
ain't been around
long enough
to know anything.

5

Foolin' a man
ain't all that hard.
Finding one that
ain't a fool
is a lot harder.

If you don't get married
you'll never have
a good man.
On the other hand,
if you ain't married
you don't need one.

Some things don't need
all the thought
people give 'em.

Oil all the wheels
on your wagon,
not just the
squeaky one.

Learn to tie some useful knots.

10

The time to dance
is when the
music's playin'.

WCCA
9/94

If a horse makes a few good moves on his own, he should be rewarded so that he will develop others.

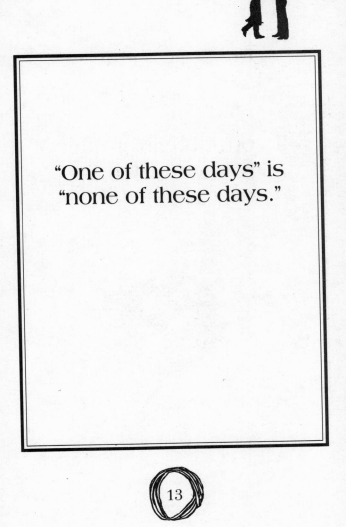

"One of these days" is
"none of these days."

If you're havin' trouble
with a mustang,
change the bit.

14

You can't get ahead
of anybody you're
tryin' to get even with.

WCCA
9/94

There's no need
to buckle on chaps
and spurs
just to drive
the milk cows in.

If you wake up and find
yourself a success,
you ain't been asleep.

17

When somebody
commences to flatterin'
you, there's generally
more up their sleeve
than just an arm.

High steppers
give bumpy rides.

19

You don't have to wait
for someone to bring
you flowers—plant
your own garden.

Be sure to
taste your words
before you
spit 'em out.

Women have
a lot of courage;
otherwise,
none would ever
get married.

You can't keep
trouble from visitin',
but you don't have to
offer it a chair.

It's prudent to spend
less time tryin' to
figure out who's right
and more time
tryin' to figure out
what's right.

If you've done it,
it ain't braggin'.

Runnin' from problems
is a sure way of
runnin' into problems.

You can't
drown your sorrows;
they know
how to swim.

27

If you find some
happiness inside
yourself,
you'll start findin' it
in a lot of
other places too.

Always remember,
it doesn't take two
to keep a secret.

If you want a little
extra attention,
ask your husband
if you can borrow
his six-shooter
for the night.

A habit is either a blessing or a curse. Think about that when you find you've fallen into one.

31

Do not shoot
at the horse;
shoot at the
jackass ridin' it.

When you get wind
of a tail,
you're following
too close.

Sheep don't associate
with wolves—and for a
dang good reason.

Cryin' about
a bad past
is a waste of
good tears.

35

Always try to make
folks happy, even if
that means going out of
your way to avoid 'em.

A fool
and his money
are soon married.

If you don't have a
good reason to do
something,
then you've got
a dang good reason
not to do it.

When you see a turtle
sittin' on a fence post,
you may not know
how it got there,
but you can be
darn sure it had help.

If you wanta say no,
it's best to say it
right away.

Don't burn down
your house
to kill a rat.

A woman's intuition
comes from payin'
attention to what's goin'
on around her.

42

There are two kinds
of people in this
ol' world;
those who believe
there are
two kinds of people,
and those who
know better.

When kissin' a
cowboy in the rain,
make sure you both
fit under his hat.

New and improved
can't beat
tried and true.

A lot of families headed
west with no more
than bedding, buckets,
Bibles, and high hopes.
That's a
pretty good start.

You'll make
better progress
if you'll
get out of
your own way.

Be wary of puppy love;
it can lead to
a dog's life.

A lesson every cowgirl
should learn
is where
her business ends
and someone
else's starts.

Never—under any circumstances—admit that you like to cook.

People whose manners
are on the absent side
are probably missin'
more than just
their manners.

51

You have to take
ranch country for
what it is, not what it
ought to be.

You can warm your
socks in the oven,
but that don't
make 'em biscuits.

Brand what needs
to be
branded.

A lot of things
that don't look good
in their raw form
turn out to be
pretty good when
they're finished.

Not all fillies ride well
the first time out.

Share your wisdom,
not your prejudices.

Don't hang your hat on someone else's peg.

There are many
kinds of bandits—
so sit on your wallet
and hold onto
your heart.

It's not what you say
to a horse
that gets its attention.
It's how you say it.

Allow no war parties
in your bed.

When you're
workin' a horse
or dealin' with a man,
take it slow,
take it easy,
and don't rush 'em.

There's no need
for a lot of talkin'
when two people
understand each other.

The secret to
a long life
is to be willin'
to grow older.

Nobody's credit is
better than
their money.

65

Crack your own whip.
Don't let anybody else
do it for you.

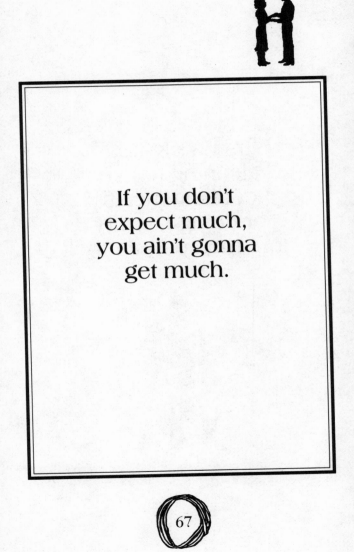

If you don't
expect much,
you ain't gonna
get much.

It's no big deal
cleaning house,
cooking meals,
or doing laundry.
More men oughta try it.

Don't find fault;
find a remedy.

About half your
troubles come from
wanting your way;
the other half
come from gettin' it.

Opportunity may
knock just once,
but temptation is a
frequent visitor.

The more inches
you give a man,
the more he
becomes a ruler.

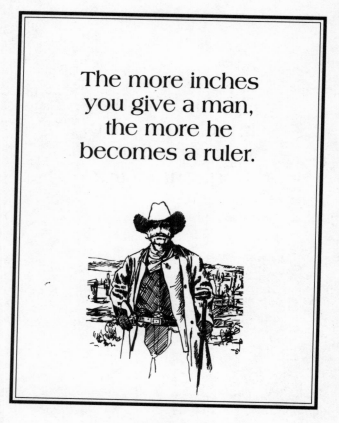

A clear conscience
is a restful pillow.

A weddin' ring should cut off the wearer's circulation.

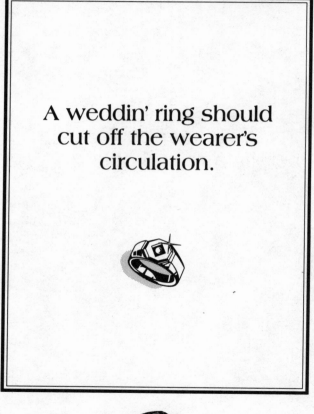

If you build walls
around yourself,
don't be surprised
if it gets kinda
lonely in there.

There's no future in livin' in the past.

If you get
all wrapped up
in yourself,
you'll find you make
a pretty small package.

It's tough
to walk away from
something you love,
but sometimes
it's the only way.

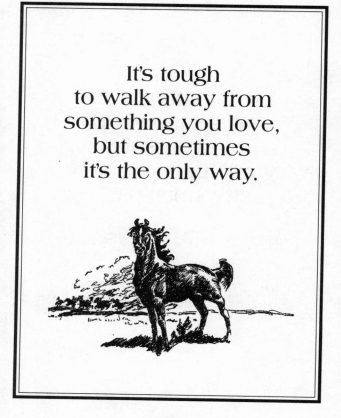

Don't try so hard
to make your man a
good husband
that you don't have
time to be a good wife.

Be sure the goin' up
is worth
the comin' down.

There is a charm
about a man
who is wild.
Don't fall for it.

Sometimes,
you just need to
take the bridle off,
throw the skillet away,
and let the
panther scream.

Don't be afraid
to ride a horse
of a different color.
Sometimes it's a nice
change of pace.

Even if it takes
more than one throw
to land a steer
and tie him,
he's still roped and tied.

Gettin' up a lynch party
is not group therapy.

85

Never show your roll.

It's easier to stay well
than to get well.

87

You can't know everything; neither can anybody else.

Nature teaches,
she never preaches.

Most everything you
hear about
a cowboy is true.
But the important thing
is—they take care of
the cows.

Charity is not a luxury
to be acquired
along the way.
It must be nurtured
from the heart's
beginning.

Always say "please"
when you tell
somebody to shut up.

Folks who have no
vices have very few
virtues.

When there's a drought everybody is dry. When it rains, everybody gets wet. Mother Nature makes no distinctions.

Most hard-boiled
people
are half-baked.

Never let yourself be drawn into a game where you do not know the rules — ALL the rules.

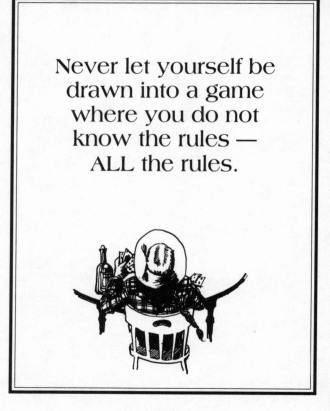

Premature ultimatums
generally result from
immature
considerations.

Never ask a man the size of his spread!

It's not a miracle
if you find an orange
under an apple tree;
something ain't right.

To win,
all you gotta do
is get up
one more time
than you fall.

Sometimes it's smart
to ask a man's advice,
but takin' it
is another matter.

Everything is better shared.

Don't let anybody's
opinion kill your
belief in yourself.

When you disagree,
try not to be
disagreeable about it.

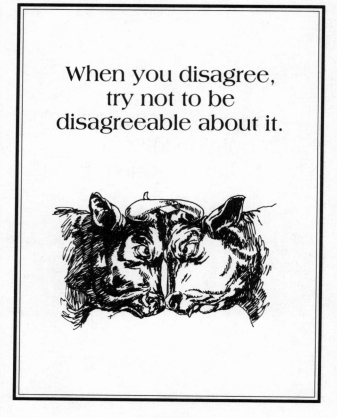

A heart must be given
to gain the
heart of another.

A promise made
is a promise kept.
That's how it is on the
cowgirl trail.

A lot of what
a man knows,
a woman knows better.

Spring calving
helps you forget
a hard winter.

Don't be afraid
to give up
on a good idea
if the facts don't
bear it out.

Before you get serious
with a cowboy, make
sure he values you
more than his truck.

Virtue is
it's own punishment.

Whenever
you go away,
always come back
before they learn to
get on without you.

Do not squander
your pity
or your strengths.

A man who wears spurs
has high expectations.
A woman who
wears spurs
has a mind of her own.

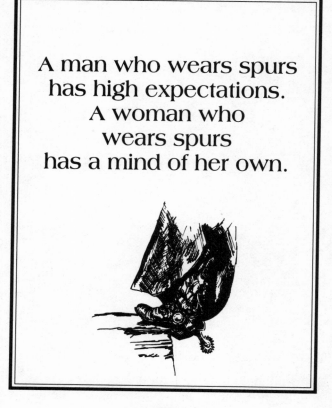

Just because a man
says it's so,
don't mean it is.

115

Ride the high country,
see through God's eyes.
Ride the desert,
feel God's strength.
Ride the prairies,
hear God's voice.

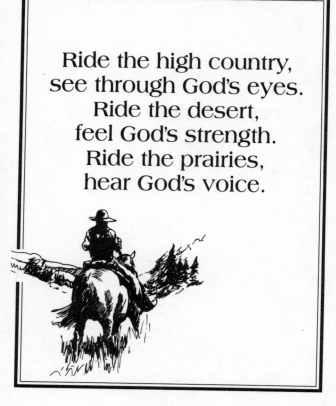

Starry nights
quiet the soul.

If you're fixin'
to get yourself
a good stallion,
don't go lookin' in the
donkey corral.

Never venture
onto thin ice
with a fancy skater.

Avoid any food
that would
gag a buzzard.

Even a fool
can be right
some of the time.

It's rōdeo,
not rodéo.

A horse is considered
well trained
when he is convinced
that he wants to do
what you want
him to do.

Keep plenty of
good hay in the barn
and you'll find it's a fact
that a smart horse
never forgets
the way home.

124

Convincing yourself
that a bad idea
is a good one,
is a bad idea.

From time to time,
find yourself
a place so peaceful
that you can
enter the quiet.

Recognizing simple
certainties can
sometimes lead
to the wildest ideas.

Once you know
where you're goin',
just climb in the saddle
and stay on the trail
'til you get there.

Given a choice
between show and tell,
silence is golden.

Avoid becoming
emotional over a
jackass.

Leisure to repent
is a luxury
ill-afforded.

A good mind
moves with the
passage of time.

There is a big
difference between
a picnic
and a pilgrimage.

Horses always start,
they never run
out of gas, and they
will not get you greasy.

A harvest
taken too early
will give you
a thin crop.

Men—
You can't live with 'em
and you can't
shoot 'em.

Baloney is baloney
no matter how thin
you slice it.

If a man thinks
that a woman who can
dog steers, ride broncs,
and rope the wind
is too much for him,
he's probably right.